MW00790764

Adam C. Laningham *M.Ed.,*
Lin Lim *Ph.D. & Val Wilson M.Ed.*

What Educators
Need to Know

Part of the Series:
Twice-Exceptional Children -
From Struggling to Thriving

A Bright Child Books LLC Publication

For more information, contact:
adam@brightchildbooks.com

BRIGHT CHILD BOOKS, LLC

BrightChildAZ.com

BOOKS, PUBLISHING, & MORE

Edited by Gayle G. Bentley
Educational Consultant, The Bentley Center

Cover art by
Adam Laningham
Eye logo by M.Gibson

A.I. was not used to write or produce any part of this book.

Contents

Acknowledgements

The authors would like to thank:

Our families for their support over the years.

All the many students with whom we have worked who have taught us to be better educators.

Purpose

The purpose of this book is to support teachers and school leaders regarding the unique needs of our twice-exceptional learners. The authors have a great wealth of experience educating and parenting these children. We hope this book will make you more aware of this vulnerable population and provide you with knowledge and practical support to help the children in your classroom or school.

This is the second book of our series, Twice-Exceptional Children: From Struggling to Thriving. Further books in the series, that are soon to be released, focus on educational strategies for the classroom, school administrators, and support for mental health professionals. The first book of the series is *What Parents Need To Know*.

We hope the series provides support for all stakeholders in the lives of 2e children and a common framework and language to support them.

Introduction

Why We Wrote This Book

As lifelong educators, Val and Adam have worked with thousands of children and families over the years. Val has worked in multiple schools, teaching gifted children from various backgrounds and at different ages. Adam has taught in several schools and served as a district-level administrator for gifted services in a large and diverse school district. As a parent of a radically accelerated, profoundly gifted daughter and a profoundly gifted and twice-exceptional (2e) son, Lin knows the parenting journey of complex outliers.

In addition, Lin is the Dean of Students and Communications at Bridges Graduate School of Cognitive Diversity in Education (BGS). She holds a Ph.D. in Human Development Psychology from Boston University, an Academic Graduate Certificate in Twice-Exceptional Education from BGS, and an Academic Graduate Certificate in Mind, Brain, and Education from Johns Hopkins University.

Fortunately, most children do just fine in our schools and become successful adults. That said, we know many children struggle in our educational system. If you are a parent of a child who is struggling, you know it can be heartbreaking for children and their families.

Many reasons result in students not thriving in school. Every child and person is unique. Some children have learning disabilities, some have difficult home lives, some have a hard time socializing, and some have unique sensory, social, emotional, and/or physical needs.

This book was written for teachers of children who have difficulty in school because of their unique learning needs due to dynamic interactions between discrepancies in area/s of high and low abilities, known as twice-exceptionality. Though the number of students who *are formally identified educationally to* fit into this category makes up a small percentage of our population, finding ways to support them tends to be quite challenging. In addition, some argue that many children unofficially fit into this category.

This book is meant to explain the complexities of 2e children in accessible ways and provide strategies to support them in their learning journey. It is meant to be a practical, easy-to-access resource for educators, based on the research and strategies three veteran gifted educators have used to support all kinds of children, including twice-exceptional, throughout their careers.

Book Study & Reflection Questions
Each chapter includes pages with questions to help the reader think about important concepts. The questions are meant to springboard the reader into a better understanding as they reflect on the content and can also serve as discussion starters for book groups. Space is intentionally left open to take notes and jot down your thoughts.

Let's get started…

Jack's Story

One of Val's Students

Jack was a third-grade student who entered my classroom during a gifted testing session one spring. (Jack is not his real name.) As the school's gifted specialist, I conducted the identification testing several times yearly. Jack was small in stature and walked into my room with an "assistant" from his classroom who was carrying his laptop for him. He presented as nervous, continuously fidgeting with a pencil in his hand. Both Jack and his "assistant" stood by the door.

"Hello, Jack," I said. "Welcome to gifted testing! May I ask who your friend is?"

"I'm afraid of heights!" he answered curtly, still near the door. My classroom was on the second floor of the school.

"I hold his laptop while he holds the railing on the stairs," said the assistant.

"Oh," I said. "Well, Jack won't need a laptop. Are you ok with taking it back with you?" The assistant nodded. I thanked her, and she left.

"I don't like stairs," said Jack.

"Well, that's ok," I said. "A lot of people do not. Go ahead and sit at this desk."

I showed him an empty desk and gave him a testing book. He nervously squeezed himself into the chair and sat fidgeting with his pencil.

After a bit more chit chat to help calm him, we proceeded with the first portion of the test. This verbal assessment section determined students' vocabulary abilities with word relationships and comprehension. Jack tackled two questions on the first portion and, with much heavy sighing and erasing of his answers, announced to me loudly and matter-of-factly that he could not read.

I challenged him to continue the test and to try his best, even if he found it difficult. He continued through each subtest and persevered, although with much sighing, erasing, and pursing of the lips. We took several breaks on this portion of the test, but this behavior continued. By the end of the verbal section, Jack had answered less than half of the questions.

Part of my role as the gifted specialist was to work with the classroom teachers to identify students showing academic potential and to assess them for gifted identification. Jack had been referred to me by his teacher on a hunch that his mathematical skills were superior to his classmates. In class, he showed excellent reasoning skills. I was not given much more information but was told that I could not take him at certain times for testing because he needed to see Ms. Smith, the reading specialist. I decided to test him in all three gifted placement areas.

As we continued with the assessment, Jack proceeded to breeze through the quantitative and logic portions of the test without incident. After scoring the sections, Jack had a high placement score in the quantitative portion, qualifying him for gifted math services. However, he scored significantly lower in the verbal section. I was not surprised at the scores after watching him take the test.

A short time later, Jack's parents received his gifted placement letter. Jack then found me in the hallway and followed me to the stairs.

"I'm in gifted! I'm in gifted! I love math. I'm really, really good in math! I know how to do lots of stuff!" he yelled as we moved down the hallway.

"Welcome to the gifted program, Jack," I told him. "You are an awesome student, and I will see you shortly. I am so glad to have you join our class!"

"I know how to do things, I really do!" he said, almost trying to convince me of his abilities.

I remember him smiling at me with a huge grin and walking backward to class doing a little dance.

As I came to know Jack better, the mathematical brilliance was quite apparent. One instance that stands out in my mind to this day was when I casually mentioned that I needed to pick a number sequence for an iPad lock with five numbers on it. He created an entire list of combinations I could employ and then wrote a formula for it "just in case I needed it."

Overall, Jack did very well in our accelerated gifted math class. However, even in math class, I observed a significant disconnect with sound relationships in his reading abilities when we worked on word problems. In some cases, he would confuse letters altogether. Working with the classroom teacher and reading specialist, I realized that Jack read at a K-1st grade level. His reading abilities had shown little growth, which proved challenging with real-world math projects or word problems in our class early on.

There was also the mantra that he often expressed. "I can't read," he would often say, even without looking at the words, or "Can you help me do this?" even before he started a project. Jack began gifted class with an immense desire to learn. His difficulties with reading and the psychological baggage that comes with a chronic lack of achievement could have easily made him unsuccessful despite his math talents. Coupled with some family issues in his early formative years and many experiences with educators who only focused on his challenges, Jack had learned to be "helpless" and an under-achiever who made many mistakes. Sometimes, he would become explosive in social situations with a more outgoing peer, feeling like the child was "taking control." As I began to work with Jack more, my three areas of concern for him were his reading ability, low self-esteem, and behavior in certain social situations. Still, Jack was brilliant in math, and that was a fact!

We learned to best serve Jack by working as a team, teaching him coping skills and how to challenge himself. The reading specialist and I brainstormed some reading strategies that helped him build on his strength of logic. For instance, the reading specialist found several games that used context clues for unknown words. He did well because of the puzzle-like format and was able to raise his vocabulary level. The school counselor started seeing him in groups. He learned several tools to use when feeling overwhelmed, such as expressing his emotions in "color words" and using relaxation techniques.

In my room, he realized that he could read "most things" (I used math projects with him that I re-wrote at a reading level slightly higher than his) and that making mistakes while learning was required. Perseverance was encouraged consistently.

"You cannot learn new things if you do not make mistakes, Jack," I said after hearing his "Will you help me do this?" for a third time in class. "In fact, Jack," I said, "you are now required to make two mistakes every time you are in my room."

It became a game after that. He would have to tell me something he did not know how to do before he left, and I would share the same. Despite it being silly in some cases, it eventually became "ok" not to know how to do something. In some cases, it became a challenge to find out as well! Eventually, Jack's confidence grew, and he learned to tackle reading difficulties and "mess up" without so much anxiety.

Over the course of three years with Jack, he was eventually diagnosed with dysgraphia and was placed on medication to help with his anxiety levels. We also built his reading abilities and increased his reading level to 4th grade. He thrives in mathematics and works an entire grade level above his school-age peers. He even competed and placed in a national math competition. Not everything in Jack's world is perfect, but Jack continues to thrive through team efforts despite his disabilities.

Working together, we were able to support his gifts as well as areas of weakness. This is what has allowed him to succeed in school and hopefully beyond.

Jack's Story

Book Study & Reflection Questions

Reflect on Jack's story. What caught your attention?

Do you have any students similar to Jack? List them and what you see as their areas of strength and areas of struggle.

What strategies help support them?

What are some areas of strength and weakness you have? How do you support or cope with them in your own life?

Chapter 1
Who Are We?

Children and individuals are all unique. Yet, despite our understanding of human uniqueness, we often need to group or categorize ourselves and others into groups for various reasons. We then assign different attributes and characteristics to those in these groups. The education field is no different.

The problem is that only some in that group share the assigned traits, and we also have individuals who fit into multiple groups. This is undoubtedly the case with Twice-exceptional (2e) children.

Sally Reis, Susan Baum, and Edith Burke published a commonly cited operational definition of 2e learners. The definition resulted from deliberations from a National Commission on Twice Exceptional Learners with different stakeholder input, including researchers, university professors, K-12 schools, psychologists, educational therapists, national and state association presidents, and graduate students.

Their definition is as follows:

Twice-exceptional learners are students who demonstrate the potential for high achievement or creative productivity in one or more domains such as math, science, technology, the social arts, the visual, spatial, or performing arts or other areas of human productivity AND who manifest one or more disabilities as defined by federal or state eligibility criteria.

These disabilities include specific learning disabilities, speech and language disorders, emotional/behavioral disorders, physical disabilities, Autism Spectrum Disorders (ASD), or other health impairments, such as Attention Deficit/Hyperactivity Disorder (ADHD). These disabilities and high abilities combine to produce a unique population of students who may fail to demonstrate either high academic performance or specific disabilities. Their gifts may mask their disabilities, and their disabilities may hide their gifts.

Identification of twice-exceptional students requires comprehensive assessment in both the areas of giftedness and disabilities, as one does not preclude the other. Professionals from both disciplines should conduct identification and, when possible, by those with knowledge about twice exceptionality to address the impact of co-morbidity of both areas on diagnostic assessments and eligibility requirements for services.

Educational services must identify and serve both the high achievement potential and the academic and social-emotional deficits of this population of students. Twice-exceptional students require differentiated instruction, curricular and instructional accommodations and/or modifications, direct services, specialized instruction, acceleration options, and opportunities for talent development that incorporate the effects of their dual diagnosis.

Twice-exceptional students require an individual education plan (IEP) or a 504 accommodation plan with goals and strategies that enable them to achieve at a level and rate commensurate with their abilities. This comprehensive education plan must include talent development goals, as well as compensation skills and strategies to address their disabilities and their social and emotional needs.

In summary -

The term 2e is a label created to classify individuals who are both gifted and have special learning needs. In other words, these children have an academic gift in one or more areas but also have a disability in one or more areas. Such children *learn differently* due to the interactions between their areas of high and low ability(s).

Being in just one of these groups (either gifted or special needs) can be very challenging for any child. For example, a child who is identified as gifted may have to overcome the expectations placed on them by having this term used for their abilities. Does being gifted mean you should be earning good grades? This is still a prevalent myth. Also, gifted children are often gifted in a particular area, yet overly high expectations may be placed on them in multiple academic areas. Understanding giftedness is still an area that we are working on to help parents and educators.

A student with a disability also has to overcome those disabilities as well as any stigmas, labels, and or expectations that are placed on them. Each label comes with certain expectations, challenges, and judgment. Working through this can be challenging for any child.

Complexities of being twice-exceptional

Susan Baum, a pioneer in 2e understanding and teaching strategies, came across many bright children in special education, and it became her passion to find ways to nurture and understand such children for success. She used color metaphors* to help others better understand the complexities of 2e learners.

2e learners are always green, a color that emerges when you mix yellow (high ability) and blue (low/disability). "It is not easy being green," she often reminds our graduate school students.

Building on Susan's work, we created our logo on the cover of this book. We hope the colors combined into the eye help to illustrate that we are learning to see the whole 2e child.

You cannot truly see the 2e child without addressing both colors. Once we see the whole child, we need to support them by leading with their areas of strength.

To read more about the work of Susan Baum and view a color visual visit: https://2ecenter.org/definitions-and resources/

Lin has since built upon Susan Baum's work to synthesize her 2e color metaphor through the lens of the N.E.S.T! perspective*, which is informed theoretically by dynamic systems as a contemporary approach to understand 2e individuals' human development across time. In other words, who we are at any point in time is always the composite of interactions between our inner and outer worlds.

The N.E.S.T! perspective offers a paradigm shift and advocates for always **leading with your child's strengths** while considering how disability(s) interact with successfully accomplishing each learning goal. This concept is very important, so we wanted to include the overview here. We have more resources that go into this concept much more in-depth. This echoes Dr. Ross Greene's starting point that all children do well if they can. Therefore, when children struggle, we should view it as an indication that something is preventing them from doing well.

More about the N.E.S.T! perspective and Lin's academic work can be found online **zenliving.com**

What are some general characteristics of twice-exceptional children?

Our friends at the Gifted Development Center developed a checklist* for recognizing common characteristics of 2e children.

This checklist is used as a screener to determine if formal assessments might be helpful. Assessments by professionals, well trained in understanding 2e complexities, form important support teams for families.

We have summarized some of the general characteristics of 2e learners taken from their checklist on the following page. You can also find the complete checklist on their website.

General Characteristics of a 2e Learner

- Appears smarter than grades or test scores suggest
- Has a sophisticated speaking vocabulary but poorer written expression
- Participates well in class discussions but does not follow through with implementation
- Has uneven academic skills, inconsistent grades, and test scores
- Does well when given sufficient time, but performs poorly on timed tests and takes much longer to complete assignments and homework than other students
- Studies very hard before tests, gets good grades on tests but soon forgets most of the learned information. Needs to restudy it for later tests
- Has excellent problem-solving skills but suffers from low self-esteem
- Excels in one area or subject but may appear average in others
- Performs well with challenging work but struggles with easy material
- Is better with reading comprehension than with phonetic decoding of words
- Is better at math reasoning than computation
- Has wonderful ideas but has difficulty organizing tasks and activities
- Has facility with computers, but illegible or slow handwriting
- Has a remarkable (sometimes bizarre) sense of humor and may use it to distract the class
- Thrives on complexity but has difficulty with rote memorization
- Understands concepts quickly and gets frustrated with the performance requirements
- Fatigues easily due to the energy required to compensate

gifted
development center
embracing giftedness

Chapter 1

Book Study & Reflection Questions

Based on the definition of twice-exceptional (2e), have you had students in your class that may fit into this definition but were not identified? List a few and what makes you think they were 2e.

What did these students struggle with, and what strategies and supports seemed to help them?

What did they do well or excel in?

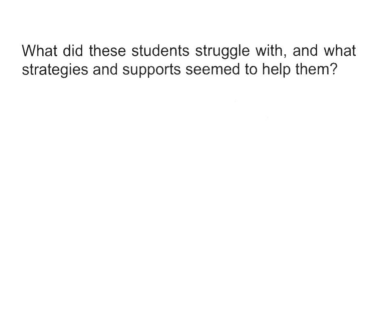

Chapter 2
Some Familiar Names

Being a twice-exceptional child (2e) has many challenges. However, by focusing on the learner's strengths and using successful coping strategies, disabilities and challenges can be effectively managed. A 2e individual can undoubtedly lead a successful life despite the issues they may struggle with.

What follows are a few examples of well-known people who have impacted our lives. The men and women we highlight in this chapter were successful individuals who were incredibly intelligent and talented but overcame significant obstacles.

Agatha Christie

Agatha Christie wrote 66 detective novels, 14 short story collections, the play *Mousetrap*, and six novels under the pseudonym Mary Westmacott. She was honored in the Guinness Book of World Records as the best-selling fiction writer of all time. But unknown to some, Agatha suffered from dysgraphia, a disorder that affects a person's ability to write and spell.

Agatha once said that writing and spelling were very difficult for her, and she was considered "slow" in school and by her family. However, she later stated in an interview that she found other ways to achieve her dreams. Her challenge with writing did not stop her from becoming a famous writer known worldwide.

Winston Churchill

Winston Churchill was the Prime Minister of Great Britain and the winner of the 1953 Nobel Prize in Literature. He served as the Prime Minister during WWII and from 1951 to 1955. Churchill was best known for his wartime leadership and eloquent radio speeches, providing encouragement and inspiration to fight against the odds, no matter how bleak the future seemed.

Ironically, he suffered from a lisp, which was rumored to be more pronounced during stressful times. He compensated by doing speech exercises and slowing down while talking.

Walt Disney

Walt Disney was the creator of Disneyland, Walt Disney World, and many beloved films and animated characters, such as Mickey Mouse. He was an entrepreneur who became a great writer, animator, and film producer, among his many talents. He holds the record for receiving the most Academy Awards and has been presented with two Golden Globes and an Emmy. His fanciful creations are beloved by children around the world.

Walt had dyslexia, which can impact a person's reading, spelling, and writing abilities. As a child, he was considered "slow" and lost a newspaper job for what they called his "lack of creativity." Little did they know that this man would become one of the creators of the world's most loved fantasy places.

Thomas Edison

Thomas Edison was an inventor and businessman who developed several ideas and devices in electric power, mass communication, sound recordings, and film. He invented the concept of the phonograph and the early light bulb, which paved the way for the world of technology we know today. His use of the scientific method in his work and his collaborations with other researchers produced some remarkable inventions.

Edison suffered from hearing problems and was nearly deaf by the age of 12. His mother worked with him, teaching him the art of patience and perseverance. He remains one of our greatest and most prolific inventors.

Albert Einstein

Albert Einstein was a theoretical physicist. He developed the theory of relativity, creating his famous equation "E=mc2", and contributed to the theory of quantum mechanics. He received the 1921 Nobel Prize for Physics.

Albert is suspected of having some autistic traits, and many believe he may have had ADHD due to his persistent struggles in school. He did not speak until he was three years old. However, his challenges did not prevent him from becoming one of the greatest physicists of all time.

Alexander Graham Bell

Alexander Graham Bell, who struggled with dyslexia, was the founder of the Bell Telephone Company and the inventor of the telephone. His grandfather and brother had worked in elocution and speech, and his mother and wife were deaf, resulting in Bell's interest in working with hearing devices and acoustics.

He first experimented with a machine that could draw shapes based on sound waves. However, with his theory that metal reeds could be tuned to convert undulating currents into sound, he later expounded upon the telegraph and experimented with acoustic telegraphy. This ground-breaking experimentation resulted in the early telephone. Alexander Graham Bell is an excellent example of what someone can do despite their challenges.

Helen Keller

Helen Keller was a political activist and lecturer. She lost her sight and hearing as an infant. After meeting her teacher, Anne Sullivan, she learned language, reading, and writing through Braille and the Tadoma method, which involves touching someone's face to perceive their jaw movements.

She attended Radcliffe and Harvard and became the first deaf and blind person to earn a Bachelor of Arts Degree. She toured the world and advocated for persons with disabilities.

Howard Hughes

Howard Hughes was an investor, engineer, and pilot. As a pilot, he set several speed records in airplanes he had designed himself. In 1935, he set a speed record of over 352 miles per hour near California in a plane called the H-1 Racer. He also contributed to the growth of transcontinental airlines and modern jet planes.

Howard suffered from chronic pain caused by several plane crashes and demonstrated eccentric behavior believed to be Obsessive Compulsive Disorder (OCD). Despite these challenges, he became highly influential and financially successful during most of his adult life.

Chapter 2

Did it surprise you that any of these people were on this list? Who stood out and why?

Can you think of any other well-known people who may likely be twice-exceptional? Who?

Why would it be important for our twice-exceptional children, or any child, to know some of these famous people?

Why is it necessary for teachers and parents to learn their stories?

Chapter 3
Where Are We?

Everywhere.

Twice-exceptional (2e) children are found in all schools and grade levels. 2e children become 2e adults, parents, uncles, aunts, and grandparents. There are three subgroups of 2e learners. Some have:

1. Gifts compensating for their disability(s)
2. A disability(s) overshadowing their gifts
3. Gifts and disability(s) masking each other

Within the educational setting, 2e learners are often identified as having gifted or special needs, with the latter being the more prevalent identification. Some children are identified in both areas and have all their needs met. Many are not identified in either area and use their own strategies to cope with school. Other 2e learners need clarification about why and how they differ from peers, and they internalize the differences as character flaws.

Any child with a disability or challenge can be talented or gifted in another area. If you understand the gifted learner, you know they are not gifted in all domains and can still struggle in certain areas. The issue is that for students who have significant struggles and are gifted, where do they fit? How do parents and educators meet their needs? How might we meet all of their needs?

2e learners tend to be under-identified and require a unique level of servicing that the regular school system needs to be equipped to identify and provide. This makes it even more difficult for these students. 2e learners can be found within every socio-economic, racial, and cultural background. When we consider that 2e learners can be found in every type of educational setting, how many 2e options are available in our schools? When looking at gifted programs and services, many schools have limited support for those learners, if any.

So, just how many children in our country are 2e? One 2006 study by the NEA estimated around 360-610,000 students might be 2e. Unfortunately, there is little overall data on what percentage of the gifted population is twice-exceptional. In fact, there are many issues in accurately determining the number of gifted students in the United States as, in the end, every state has its own definition of giftedness and how it is measured.

Based on quantitative data, we can only assume how many students formally fit into the 2e category. Linda Silverman, an eminent clinician of complex outliers, states that giftedness masks disabilities and disabilities depress intelligence test scores. The public school system currently has approximately 3.2 million gifted and talented students. Around 6 million students are also being served by the Individuals with Disabilities Act. With that in mind, around 6% of this population is most likely gifted and talented, based on the numbers.

There needs to be a more accurate way to identify 2e students, and then we can develop an appropriate program model to serve them.

Chapter 3

Once you know that there are likely to be twice-exceptional learners in your classroom, whether formally diagnosed or not, will this impact the choices you make in your classroom? How?

Is your school offering support for these types of learners? How are they supported?

Reflect and describe how their academic needs are met.

How are their social and emotional needs met?

Chapter 4
Problems We Face in a School Setting

The first problem these students face is having adults understand that they can be gifted or talented in one or more areas while simultaneously struggling in another area. **The second challenge is the ability of the school system to provide everyone with an education that meets their academic and emotional needs while assisting them in reaching their potential.**

Twice-exceptional means that a learner has gifts and talents and a disability in one or more areas.

Let's begin with some disabilities these students may have. Some of the more common twice-exceptionalities are as follows:

· Learning Challenges

· Physical Challenges

· Sensory Challenges

· Autism Spectrum Disorder

- Emotional and Behavior Disorders

- AD/HD

- Dyslexia

According to the *Twice Exceptional Dilemma* from the National Education Association, twice-exceptional students often face the following challenges in the public school system:

1. Identified as gifted but not having an identified disability
   (gifts compensate for disability)

2. Identified as having a disability but not having an area of giftedness
   (disability overshadows gifts)

3. Not identified as either, with one exceptionality masking the other
   (gifts and disability mask each other)

The public school system is structured with three main ways to service children:

- The traditional route, which lends to the "average" student

- The special education route, which assists those students demonstrating a disability or challenge in their learning

- The gifted route, which serves students with an academic or other strength

The traditional assessments that are in place for these structures are not specifically equipped to discover a student with a dual, specialized diagnosis. In addition, educators and school administrators are often not given adequate training to identify or provide instruction to these students.

Families may also be unaware of their needs because they lack knowledge of the characteristics of a dual diagnosis and because of the ability of the gifted traits and disabilities to mask one another.

As a result, many twice-exceptional children are under-identified and are left to struggle on their own.

For instance, a student who has been identified as gifted but has an unidentified disability can struggle with the following issues:

- Self-esteem and motivational issues due to challenges in learning and misguided expectations of others

- Being labeled an underachiever based on lack of work or struggles with executive functioning*

- Lack of services or appropriate differentiation because of under-identified challenges

- Emotional and behavioral issues that surface because of the lack of support in the areas of need

*Higher level cognitive processes of planning, decision-making, problem-solving, action sequencing, task assignment and organization, effortful and persistent goal pursuit, inhibition of competing impulses, flexibility in goal selection, and goal-conflict resolution.

-American Psychological Association Dictionary

Likewise, a student who has been identified with a disability but has not been identified as gifted has the following challenges:

- Boredom due to lack of challenge in areas of strength

- Test scores that do not adequately reflect strengths and giftedness

- Underserved talents and strengths due to a high level of remediation

- Low expectations of self, family, and educators

- Low self-esteem

- Learned helplessness

In some cases, students challenged in either of these scenarios may appear "typical" because they have learned to hide and accommodate their shortcomings.

In any case, 2e students need an appropriate education that assists them with their giftedness as well as disability or area of challenge.

Fortunately, this is becoming a more widely known area of need. More research is starting to focus on supporting students facing these challenges.

We focus on students who come into classrooms with challenges that coexist with their giftedness. We have an entire book with strategies on how to support gifted children. There is a summary of strategies on the following page.

Looking at these two focus areas in one individual, we understand that these students genuinely need extra understanding and support.

Gifted & Trauma – 20 Things Adults Need to Know

From Gifted Children & How Trauma Impacts Them by Adam Laningham, Melissa Sadin, & Nathan Levy

1. Please Do Not Use The "G" Word With Me

2. Please Do Not Assume Labeling Me Will Help Me

3. Just Because I Have The Potential To Excel At Things Does Not Mean That I Will Want To

4. I Am Not A Tutor Or Teacher Assistant

5. Writing Is Sometimes Hard For Me

6. Sometimes I May Seem Lazy, But Other Times I Am Just Not Motivated

7. Just Because I Am Academically Above My Average Age Level Peers Does Not Mean I Am As Socially Mature As They Are

8. Just Because I Am Smart Does Not Mean I Am Organized

9. Sometimes I Just Know Things

10. I Still Need To Acquire Basic Knowledge

11. School Is Not Designed For Kids Like Me & Gifted Does Not Mean I Like Or Will Do Well In School

12. I Have My Passions That I Must Explore - I Do Not Know Why I Become Fixated On Certain Topics, Or Why My Interests Change

13. My Brain Is Motivated By Novelty

14. I Am The Most Engaged When I See The Big Picture

15. I Often Need True Differentiation

16. Please Do Not Stop Me From Questioning Things

17. I Need To Be Taught How To Think And Problem-Solve

18. Connections, Connections, Connections

19. Please Take A Breath, I Am Going To Be Just Fine

20. We Really Need The 50 / 50 Rule for Our Gifted Programs

BRIGHT CHILD
—— B O O K S ——
www.BrightChildBooks.com

Find many more books or book a training on our website:

www.brightchildbooks.com

Chapter 4

Book Study & Reflection Questions

What specific challenges or lack of support may a 2e student face at your school?

What systems do you already have in place that would benefit these learners?

If you have a 2e student struggling, who would you be able to go to in search of support?

Chapter 5
Challenges Faced by Our Parents

Understanding a child's needs can be quite frustrating when they are struggling both at home and at school. These children can seem so bright in one moment or a particular area and then appear to crumble in the next. It is difficult to understand the dichotomy and find help and support when parents have difficulty understanding what the issue really is.

Parents need to overcome many complexities when it comes to raising twice-exceptional children. Over the years, we have noticed the following most common complexities:

Identification complexities- Identifying the actual needs of their child can be quite difficult for parents. The federal government does not mandate gifted programs; thus, they vary from state to state and even from school to school. Identifying these students as having special needs typically occurs much faster, as special education services are federally mandated. Areas of struggle often seem more straightforward to identify and support than areas of strength. Because of this, talents may be overlooked in the school setting because of the attempts to support areas of deficiency.

Program complexities - Because the content of gifted programs is left to the discretion of the state, the district, and, in some cases, the individual school, not all programs are as rigorous as they could be, and not all teachers are fully trained. Often, they are not equipped to handle the twice-exceptional student. Teachers need to understand how to use strength-based strategies while accommodating challenges that may impede successful task completion.

Social and Emotional - Twice-exceptional children are exceptional beings with complex needs. They can become more easily frustrated, have low self-esteem, and become isolated because of misunderstandings. We must facilitate twice-exceptional children to become self-aware and self-reliant, eventually advocating for their own needs.

Please Understand

When a parent expresses frustration with the teacher, it is important to understand that the parent may have been "in the struggle" for quite some time. Seeing your child performing poorly or feeling miserable at school is heartbreaking.

All of this may happen without:

- Knowing how to ask for help

- Understanding the problem

- Working with teachers who were not aware of the needs of 2e children or did not have strategies to help

As well as,

- Feeling they are the only ones going through frustration

- Thinking they have done something wrong in raising their 2e child

Chapter 5

Imagine you are a parent who has realized your child is 2e. What are your worries or concerns?

Imagine you are a parent; how would your child be serviced if they attended your school today?

Now that you know some of the unique challenges these parents face, how may this understanding help you work with parents in the future?

Chapter 6
Challenges Faced by Our Teachers

Teachers face an ever-increasing mountain of challenges in their profession. Many challenges, such as the recent global pandemic, political discourse and mandates from politicians and local governments, consistent budget cuts, and high teacher turnover, are, for the most part, out of their hands. Yet these amazing professionals persevere and do what is best for kids every day. Meeting the needs of every individual child in the classroom can be tough; some would say nearly impossible, even when ignoring the external challenges mentioned above.

Teachers are faced with many dilemmas regarding the needs of the 2e child. First, the 2e student may not demonstrate their gifted traits in the classroom. This can occur for many reasons.

According to Higgins, Baldwin, and Pereles' *Comparison of Students With and Without Disabilities,* they may display the following characteristics:

1. Difficulty with reading and writing but demonstrate high verbal ability

2. Demonstrate slow processing and memory skills but have high observation skills

3. Excel in critical thinking, decision-making, and questioning skills but may seem disrespectful to adults or show attention issues

4. Have strong imaginations but may appear to daydream or be out of touch

Also, when gifted students struggle in school, their identification for gifted services is sometimes questioned. Sadly, the stigma of having a challenge or disability often leads some to believe that a student is not gifted or should not be offered gifted services. This is a significant injustice to 2e students, causing them great frustration.

Teachers should be aware of and on the lookout for students who exhibit both gifts and struggles in certain areas. Disabilities in gifted students can go unnoticed for many years. This can suppress the potential of the student, both academically and emotionally.

Likewise, disabled students who exhibit talents and gifts should not be dismissed from being gifted. A student with a disability can have high aptitude in one or more areas, including nonacademic areas such as leadership, creativity, or athletics.

When faced with these types of cognitive and behavioral demonstrations, a classroom teacher may be quick to rule out the possibility of giftedness. The identification of twice-exceptional students is a complicated process. It requires an awareness of how the dual diagnosis presents itself and an enhanced ability to use assessments and identification procedures to determine the issues. A "one size fits all" assessment approach will not identify the needs of these students.

When identifying the issues surrounding these types of students, it is important to utilize a **collaborative, problem-solving approach** involving evidenced-based data and a multi-disciplinary team of professionals when a disability or giftedness is suspected. This is best practice, as it allows us to consider the learner holistically.

Once a student and their needs are identified, offering support is the next step. When considering implementing interventions, finding opportunities to nurture strengths while developing ways to scaffold challenges is critical. Support staff is often unavailable, and gifted resources are limited at best in many schools. If a teacher is fortunate enough to have the support of both special education and gifted services, the issue may then be collaboratively integrating that support.

The burden often falls on the classroom teacher. Schools need to provide trained support staff who know how to support the teacher in differentiating the curriculum and provide for these children's social and emotional needs.

Differentiation is not new to the world of education. There are countless approaches to finding different strategies to meet students' individual needs. The important thing for a teacher to remember is that all students are different, and it may take incorporating many different strategies to meet the needs of one child in one area. The good news is that the other students in the class may also benefit from these strategies.

Chapter 6

Have you encouraged your parents to share their child's strengths and areas in which they may need additional support with you? How can you do this each year?

Do you have resources that can provide you with ideas and tools to differentiate for various learners? Brainstorm here.

Who is a colleague you can work with to share ideas?* Does your school have opportunities for teachers to collaborate and share instructional strategies? If not, how can you suggest this?

Please also feel free to contact the authors of this book. We can help.

Chapter 7
Challenges Faced by Our Schools and School Districts

Identification

At the state level, identifying students with disabilities often takes a front seat compared to identifying gifted students. Individuals with disabilities are protected by federal law, and schools and districts are required to look for students who qualify and then provide them with a specialized education. The federal government funds identification and special education services.

Identification of gifted students is another matter. As of the writing of this book, there is no mandated federal support for assessing or servicing gifted students. Decisions about gifted programming are made at the state and local levels. The identification process, the provision of services, and even the definition of "gifted" varies across the board. In addition, funding for gifted services can vary significantly from district to district.

As a result, identifying a 2e student does not appear to be a high priority. It usually takes a parent or a proactive teacher to start the process, and even then, there can be delays along the way. A solid, formal process in which a 2e student can be identified and assisted is sorely lacking. Research suggests that parents seem to be the first to notice their child's 2e traits; however, parents typically do not know the school's or district's educational process to find the necessary support for their child.

If you are wondering if a student you are working with may be twice-exceptional, we have a checklist to help determine if what you notice may indicate a 2e individual. We encourage you to be proactive in advocating for the support of any student showing signs of struggle.

What are some general characteristics of twice-exceptional children?

Our friends at the Gifted Development Center developed a checklist* for recognizing common characteristics of 2e children. Please refer to Chapter 1 for the list.

This checklist can be used as a screener to determine if formal assessments might be helpful. Evaluations conducted by a professional trained in understanding 2e complexities may contribute immensely to the support for families.

Staffing

Due to the difficulty of identifying these students and the continued budget restraints of our schools, finding these students the staff support needed can be challenging. Finding specific teachers, specialists, and counselors who understand the needs of 2e children can also be laborious. However, identifying these students and advocating for their needs is a vital first step.

Often, the school will have special needs support available, but the classroom teacher will still need to provide gifted instruction. In this case, the teacher will need to be flexible in supporting all of the students' needs but pay special attention to the students' areas of strength. Some typical strategies include curriculum compacting, acceleration, and allowing students to show what they have learned by choosing their own products. More of this will be discussed in Chapter 8.

Scheduling/Flexible Grouping

Scheduling services may also be tricky, even for schools that can staff full gifted and special needs services. One key is to have teachers **flexibly group students** within their classrooms, their grade level, and outside of their grade levels as needed. Teachers can narrow their focus when addressing student needs if students can be flexibly grouped by their needs and abilities. This is especially true with math.

However, let's look at reading instruction first. Any classroom will have a range of students with different reading abilities. The students should not always be forced into one large group for instruction. Advanced students will be bored, and struggling students will be frustrated. The class should be broken into ability groups for a significant portion of their instructional reading time to meet all the students' needs better. Depending on the students' ability levels, teachers may be able to flex their groups into other classrooms at that grade level. This way, all levels can be addressed, and students can be taught in more reasonably sized groups. Teachers within the grade level need to have a scheduled time when this can occur across the classes.

Additionally, students may be ahead of their typical age peers in their comprehension abilities. To meet their needs, the students may require a pull-out service each day to provide this instruction, or they may be able to "Walk Up" to the next grade level to receive a more advanced ELA curriculum. This, too, would require two or more grade levels to schedule the subject simultaneously so that students can move into other grade levels as needed.

Flexible grouping and allowing acceleration are particularly effective strategies for advancing math instruction. Students who are gifted in math can not only grasp concepts faster and go more in-depth, but they can also move more quickly through math content. Facilitating students to move at their own pace allows them to stay at an appropriate level of challenge and can help them in other areas. If a student struggles in other areas, this opportunity to accelerate in an area of strength can be a significant confidence booster that will encourage the student to persevere in areas of struggle.

Note from Adam: In my experience, I have seen many gifted children, specifically at Title 1 schools or schools in low socioeconomic areas, languish when they were not provided appropriate support and rigor, especially when they arrived at the middle and high school levels. One of my priorities as a district manager was to make sure that gifted children with math strengths could accelerate or walk up to the next grade level if their skills/abilities indicated that it would benefit them.

Doing so gave the students an advantage during middle and high school by allowing them to shine in math. When students were a grade level or more ahead, they could take more choice or elective courses (including career and technical education) that helped them enjoy and find meaning in school. In many cases, these classes helped to open their eyes to new career opportunities when they graduated.

Training and Professional Development

Although scheduling is very important, not even the most efficient schedule can replace an outstanding, well-trained teacher. Professional development is crucial. Teachers need to be able to continue to grow and learn strategies to meet the needs of all students. They need to be provided time to work together and learn from experts.

Professional development should:

1.   Be student-focused
2.   Be based on research and experience
3.   Be focused on specific areas of need
4.   Include time to collaborate, lesson plan, reflect, and follow up

Chapter 7

Is your professional development training meeting your needs? Reflect and explain.

Do you have time to collaborate with your colleagues? How is that helpful, or how would that help?

Do you have a say in the training you receive?
Who can you talk to, and what can you do to
make your training more beneficial in meeting
your needs?

Chapter 8
Successful Strategies for Our Teachers

This chapter follows a different structure. Instead of waiting until the end of the chapter for our questions and reflections, we are leaving space for you to write down your thoughts after each strategy. This will allow you to focus on each one as you read the chapter. Questions will also be provided halfway through and at the end for further reflection.

This chapter will review a few proven strategies that may help in the classroom. We could not go into much depth here, but be on the lookout for our more in-depth strategy book the authors are currently working on. It will include topics such as dual differentiation, scaffolding, jigsaw grouping, active constructive responding, and bridging, as well as ways to leverage technology beyond assistive technology.

A gifted child with a disability or weakness in an area **regularly experiences challenges and trials** that arise because of the gap between their aptitude and their ability to demonstrate academic and social skills. This may translate to them not performing to their potential. It is essential to take a **multi-faceted approach** when providing support and services for these students.

We recommend some steps that teachers can take to make their classrooms less intimidating and more supportive for these learners. Generally, these steps can nurture a 2e student and any other student in a teacher's classroom, so they are appropriate for any teacher to implement. Space is provided after each strategy for you to write notes and reflect.

1. Build relationships with students

Students work better in school if they feel their teacher cares for them and accepts them for who they are. Gaps are bridged when a teacher takes a genuine interest in a student's strengths, weaknesses, and likes and dislikes. This does not mean a teacher has to do everything the student wants or that they can't hold the student accountable. On the contrary, teachers who are seen as tough are typically the ones the students know care the most.

Students who believe their teacher likes and values them are far more likely to engage in the learning process. Engagement often leads to more significant learning and better self-confidence.

How are you building relationships with your students now?

2. Build positive relationships among students and allow for different types of grouping

A learning environment that openly accepts and celebrates all learners and their differences provides a safe place to celebrate learning milestones and take risks. Likewise, allowing homogeneous and heterogeneous grouping facilitates students to work with peers with similar abilities to share their strengths. Classrooms should allow students to easily flow in and out of different groups and experiences (based on needs or tasks).

Even at a very young age, students know they are all different. They know they come to class with different strengths, weaknesses, and experiences. Teachers should not be afraid to show that students need different things at different times. Make this part of the culture in your classroom, and the kids will get what they need and understand it's important for everyone to get what they need. Doing this does not isolate students who need extra support; it establishes a culture for students to feel comfortable asking for help and support when needed. This is vital for our 2e learners but also suitable for all children.

How are you currently using grouping in your classroom? Can you think of ways to group your students differently or more effectively?

3. Encourage and teach organizational skills

Organizing workspaces, setting deadlines, creating study and strategic plans, practicing self-reflection, and even self-care are all tools that help students become successful and better able to take on challenging material. When students have a "toolkit" for success, they feel less overwhelmed and generally produce a better outcome in their work.

Many students need help with organization. This is something that many must be taught, and some will take quite some time to master. Direct lessons on organizing should be taught periodically.

Ensure your classroom has a good balance of structure in the behavior and task completion areas. It should have an adequate number of structured projects and activities so that students can easily follow steps and master concepts. A practical activity to incorporate this is using project-based units. These units can be engaging but also adhere to a structure and rubric that students should be able to follow to meet expectations.

Reflect on how you are teaching organizational skills. Are you doing enough? How can you incorporate more?

4. Provide direct, explicit instruction

Providing direct, explicit instruction in many areas is essential, as students need an opportunity and an example to learn new material. This new material may include academics, social-emotional issues, executive functioning strategies, self-care techniques, and the building of social support systems. It is crucial to balance direct instruction with time with the class as a whole, small learning groups, and individual learning time. The students need to have these opportunities throughout their school day.

Many teachers believe the gifted label means direct instruction is not necessary. This is simply not the case. If a child is gifted in a particular area, they may just need less direct instruction when compared to their typical-aged peers, as they can grasp the concepts more quickly with less repetition. A 2e child, or any gifted child who is not gifted in a particular area, will still need direct instruction, especially in less-preferred areas. They may even need more explicit direct instruction or more opportunities to review and learn a concept in an area of relative weakness. Getting to know each student and their individual needs is essential.

It is also necessary to ensure the student understands the directions and concepts initially. Often gifted learners think they know what to do, but in reality, they have missed something along the way. They then proceed with that project, task, or activity and experience great frustration later.

Not only do teachers need to know what a student already knows and needs to know, but they also need to check in along the way to make sure the student is on the right path. Limiting unintentional frustration is very important for teachers, especially with our 2e learners. As we have said before, they will experience frustrations as it is. Limiting unintentional frustration and carefully crafting opportunities to manage and learn from frustration is critical to support this population.

How are you doing this now?

5. Dually differentiated instruction

As educators, we need to get to know the students in our classroom. An effective teacher uses pre-assessments and experiences working with the students to help plan and differentiate instruction.

Dual differentiation is a critical instructional strategy unique to teaching twice-exceptional students. Dual differentiation refers to instruction that is differentiated after considering **both** areas of strengths and areas of challenges. We must provide accommodations and modifications to classroom material based on strengths, weaknesses, learning gaps, and learning profiles.

Teachers should scaffold with strategies, including the use of technology, as appropriate. They must teach students different ways to learn concepts, offer them opportunities to explore using hands-on instruction, experience real-world problems, participate in group projects, and experience traditional paper-pencil-type instruction.

There is no wrong type of instruction. It is only "bad" if we force learners to conform to one style. Teachers need to incorporate multiple types of instruction to meet the needs of learners as they need it.

What are some ways you are differentiating now?
What are some techniques you would like to
incorporate?

6. Teach critical and creative thinking, always encouraging curiosity

All learners, particularly gifted and 2e students, need teaching strategies that consist of open-ended, analytical, critical thinking and opportunities for problem-solving and self-evaluation. Students need these to learn how to tackle problems. Some activities that are good for this are Socratic discussions, simulations, novel studies, writing prompts, lateral thinking puzzles, and Stories with Holes.

Some twice-exceptional students experience high anxiety around learning. Encouraging curiosity is a psychologically safe way for students to become more open to critical and creative thinking activities. In addition, not all students are naturally "creative."

We currently see activities that "encourage creativity" emphasized more heavily in educational programs. Creativity is indeed valuable and a good thing to be encouraged. The issue that might arise may be an added pressure for students to be creative. The authors of this book believe the emphasis should be more on **curiosity**. Letting students honor and explore what they are curious about does not add the pressure that may arise from encouraging them to be productively creative. Most children, especially at an early age, are curious learners. Let's use their innate instinct of curiosity and honor it. Interest itself can help encourage the love of learning over a lifetime.

Teachers should also have many opportunities for unstructured activities throughout the year. These activities should allow students to be curious, explore, experiment, be creative, and learn from mistakes. A great example of an unstructured opportunity would be to incorporate problem-based learning. Problem-based learning puts the onus on the students to solve problems and gives them real-world opportunities to make decisions and possibly fail in a safe environment. It is not the teacher who "teaches" what the students need to know; it is the exploration of the students as they work to solve real-world problems while the teacher guides and coaches them through the research and problem-solving process.

How are you incorporating the strategies discussed in your classroom now?

If you now emphasize creativity in your classroom, how can you transition to an emphasis on curiosity? Brainstorm here.

7. Maintain clear communication with parents and students

Communication is incredibly important. Over the years, most issues and concerns have arisen from a lack of communication or misinformation. Make classroom expectations and policies known at the beginning of the year and expectations for large assignments when introduced. Have regular one-on-one meetings with your students to review their progress and see how they are feeling. Have conversations with them about their goals and ideas about their strengths and challenges.

Parents are your support team and your cheerleaders! We all want the same thing - children to be successful in school and life. Be available for parent-teacher conferences throughout the year and bring parents into the classroom to help with activities, events, and small group instruction.

Technology makes communication more manageable, so take advantage of it. You can survey your families at the beginning of the school year and see how and how often they would like to communicate. Many excellent teachers keep websites up to date, send weekly emails home, or use other apps to stay in contact with their students' families. Whichever way you choose to communicate, be sure to keep parents and guardians informed on classroom news, studies, and events.

How are you communicating with families now?

What can you do to increase communication in a time-efficient way?

8. Be aware of physical, social, and emotional aspects of the classroom that can be barriers to learning

Neuroscience research demonstrates the close connection between our mind, brain, and body.
When a student is struggling, teachers should be aware that the classroom's physical, social, and/or emotional aspects may be the cause or a contributing factor. Paying attention to possible physical, social, and emotional aspects of the classroom can help enhance learning for your students.

How is your classroom currently set up?

Can you think of ways to make your classroom more functional or aesthetically engaging for your students? Brainstorm some ideas here.

In A Twice-Exceptional Friendly Classroom, Teachers:

1. Build relationships with students

2. Build positive relationships among students and allow for different types of grouping

3. Encourage and teach organizational skills

4. Provide targeted, direct instruction

5. Dually-differentiate instruction

6. Infuse critical and creative thinking and always encourage curiosity

7. Maintain clear communication with parents and students

8. Are aware of physical, social, and emotional aspects of the classroom that can **be barriers to learning**

Twice-Exceptional Children - From Struggling to Thriving

In A Twice-Exceptional Friendly Classroom, Teachers:

Reflect on the list. Overall, how are you doing? What area(s) do you need to focus on?

Focus on one or two areas. Brainstorm some ideas to help you improve in those areas.

An Education Plan

Whether or not a student has been identified, it is important to develop an education plan to nurture a student's gifts and support their challenges. There are varied ways to plan for a student's individual needs. Some are much more structured, and others are more open-ended. It can be a formal process or more fluid, depending on the student's needs or your school's requirements.

If you are just getting started or would like to evaluate a plan you are currently using, what follows are some steps to develop a well-rounded plan. As you read, please use the steps to reflect and improve on a plan already in place or when preparing a new one.

1. Determine the student's strengths, interests, and challenges
This can be done through school data, formal and informal assessments, interest surveys, and multiple intelligence information. It can also be done through interviews with the family and questions about performance outside of school. It is important to always include the child in this data gathering, no matter their age.

The point is that teachers use multiple sources to gain a good understanding of the child. Teachers should also review information gathered over a comprehensive period from different sources. Children constantly grow, learn, adapt, and cope with varying life stressors. We need a broad and diverse data set over time to get the most accurate picture.

What are some other ways you can determine a student's abilities?

Are there other adults who could provide valuable input from interactions throughout the day or over more extended periods of time? List them and how they may help.

2. Identify one strength and one focus point

A student may have multiple areas that need to be addressed. They may have several areas of struggle that need extra support. It is important to be aware of all of these; however, you should choose one strength and one challenge to create an educational plan around. Selecting one of each keeps the focus and will less likely overwhelm the student (and teachers). Remember, it is always important to lead with a child's strength!

What are some typical areas you think will need to be addressed?

3. Identify, from various other experts, ideas to assist with the educational plan

It is important to identify the people who will play a role in the instructional plan. Experts can include classroom teachers, gifted specialists, special education specialists, psychologists, counselors, parents, other experts in the field, and school administrators. Don't forget about the child. The child should always be included in the process, regardless of age. They can provide valuable input and will have more buy-in for the plan if they are included.

These experts can collaborate to develop the plan. They can help monitor its success, help to see the whole picture, and measure student growth. Also, be sure to consider the child's friends and siblings. They can also be a great resource to get the whole picture of your child. The writers of this book also are available for consultations, training, and support by email, phone, or in-person training.

Who else should be included in the process?

4. Explore all avenues to meet individual needs

Differentiation in the regular classroom and formal special or gifted education services should be considered during school hours. After-school opportunities, such as clubs, sports, and independent study, should also be considered as additional support.

List some things that are likely to help.

5. Develop the Educational Plan
The plan should have specific, measurable goals with prescribed interventions, enrichment activities, and benchmark dates for review. Those providing regular instruction, interventions, or enrichment in any area should be identified. The frequency and duration of their instructional methods and progress monitoring should also be recorded. Accommodations and/or modifications should also be illustrated in the plan.

Write down some goals here.

6. Review and adjust the plan as needed

The plan can be altered at any time, depending on achievement or needed remediation. If you review the plan and the child is not showing improvement, it is important to collaborate, adjust, and try new interventions.

If the child has shown improvement in the area that was the focus and met the goal, it is time to adjust or develop a new plan to support another area(s). **Please make sure to share the success and data with the child.** This feeling of success can be used in the future when the child begins to focus on an area of struggle. Identifying strategies that worked in the past and remembering the feelings of success can be powerful tools to help motivate and lead to success in the future.

How will you review the plans, and how will you know when they need to be adjusted? How will you include the student in the process and evaluation?

Once the plan has been developed, then it can be implemented, focusing on a strength-based approach. This can be done by nurturing strengths to counter-balance challenges through an intervention process in which instruction is tailored to the student. Providing interventions and enrichment that will help strengthen the student in academics or social-emotional areas will help fill any learning gaps.

One key to ensuring that interventions and differentiation occur is setting up a classroom structure with adequate time for group and individual learning time. When students have clear expectations and are trained to self-monitor and be engaged in their learning, it frees the teacher to support different student needs simultaneously. When students are working on various tasks that have been planned ahead of time based on their needs, more levels of instruction can occur, and more student needs can be met efficiently.

The educational plan and its implementation must be monitored closely to determine its effectiveness and ability to meet the student's needs. One or more modifications may be needed during the school year as the student needs them.

 # Steps In an Education Plan to Nurture a Student's Gifts & Support Their Challenges:

1. Determine the student's strengths, interests, and challenges

2. Identify one strength and one focus point of challenge

3. Identify important experts to assist with the educational plan

4. Explore all avenues to meet individual needs

5. Develop the educational plan

6. Review and adjust the plan as needed

Twice-Exceptional Children - From Struggling to Thriving

Reflect on the list. Overall, how are you doing with this concept? What area(s) do you think you need to focus on?

Chapter 8

Book Study & Reflection Questions

What other pieces might you need to make the process discussed effective at your school?

Brainstorm some ideas to make the process
discussed more effective at your school.

Chapter 9
Successful Strategies for Our Schools

This is another more in-depth chapter. Like Chapter 8, we leave space for you to write your thoughts after each section. This will allow you to focus on each one as you read the chapter. Questions will also be provided at the end for further reflection.

Schools should have several modes of identification when trying to identify twice-exceptional students. Different types of assessments and observations can be utilized to obtain the whole picture of a student's learning style and abilities. This process could include formal and informal modes of evaluation, as well as anecdotal records. Schools should have a defined service model that provides challenging instruction with adaptations and modifications where needed. If this does not serve its purpose, self-contained rooms utilizing a gifted or special education model may be used.

Programs must be flexible regarding which students enter or exit certain services if needed. Previews of educational plans in place should take place at least once a year with appropriate stakeholders. Teachers, administrators, and parents must collaborate and communicate regularly about short and long-term goals, instruction and adaptations, tiered learning, evaluations, and resources.

One of the ways to successfully service and monitor any student's progress is through a Response to Intervention (RTI) tiered approach. There are different versions of this, but their fundamentals are valuable. Some general tiers can be described as follows:

Tier One

Tier One occurs in the regular classroom. General instruction is provided to all students. It addresses the grade level standards and offers formative and summative assessments, along with some differentiation, to measure achievement and provide scaffolding.

What does this look like in your school?

Tier Two

Tier Two occurs in small groups and consists of supplemental instruction that complements core instruction. This instruction can be enrichment or remediation based on the student's needs. Tier Two also includes differentiation, assessments, and benchmarks to determine success. The regular classroom teacher or a specialist can deliver this level. One of the best ways to do this in the classroom is by creating a consistent time for learning center activities multiple times a week. Learning centers are when students can work in small groups on different activities while the teacher pulls small groups of students to support specific learning goals.

When the students are used to the rules and procedures for this activity, they can work in groups while the teacher can focus on a group or individual to support targeted needs. This may take some time at the beginning of the year to ensure students understand the routines and procedures. Sometimes, it takes quite a bit of time for them to become more independent and work in centers, but this can be employed at any grade level. Teachers who succeed with this have put in time at the beginning of the year and enjoy the benefits of small group instruction for the rest of the school year.

What does this look like in your school? How are
the teachers trained and supported in small-group
instruction?

Tier Three

Tier Three is implemented when a student does not demonstrate mastery of a standard or learning expectation after the Tier Two interventions. A specialist usually provides these interventions or enrichment. Many schools have specialists that cover this tier. These students need one-on-one instruction. If this is an area of remediation, typically, a reading specialist or special needs teacher can provide the intervention. Sometimes, this is an area of great strength, and the student may need coaching with a gifted specialist.

What does this look like in your school? If you do not have a specialist for a given area, who can support students in this role?

Grouping Gifted Students

One basic service or model is always to group gifted-identified students for a portion, if not the majority, of the school day. Students need to be able to find and work with peers who have similar talents and abilities. This can be done using a "Cluster Model" in which all gifted and 2e students are grouped in one classroom at each grade level.

A lot of information is available on how to appropriately group or cluster gifted children. The work by the late and wonderful Marsha Gentry can be particularly helpful. Also, look for more support and resources from Bright Child AZ, which will be available in the future.

Another service, which can be done in conjunction with the cluster model, is offering pull-out services for gifted students in specific subject areas or enrichment blocks. This requires a specialist in gifted education to provide enrichment or instruction for these students. This structure, combined with clustering, can easily fit into the RTI model.

How are you grouping students at your school?
How are the teachers supported? How can it be
improved?

The Role of Talent Development

Providing an opportunity for all students to identify and develop their talents is essential in supporting their unique needs and gifts. This is especially true for the 2e student. In the world of 2e, there is a considerable time commitment for learning to modify and strategize for their learning challenges. However, just as much time should be spent on discovering and developing their talents. We cannot overlook the gifted in the twice-exceptional learner if we want them to succeed in school and life.

Interest surveys or exploratory activities to encourage self-discovery are simple ways to help find their gifts and talents. Providing mentorships, independent study experiences, field trips, clubs, and project development opportunities can also allow these children to expand and develop their skills.

How are you currently implementing talent development in your classroom? How can you provide more of this to all of your students?

The Role of STEM, STEAM, & CTE

STEM (Science, Technology, Engineering, & Math), STEAM (Science, Technology, Engineering, Arts, & Math), & CTE (Career and Technical Education) programs, when done well, are excellent at providing hands-on, meaningful experiences for all students. Gifted and special needs students can find these classes, programs, and activities vital to keep them engaged, find meaning in their studies, and allow them to feel successful.

Science, Technology, Engineering, & Math-

These programs seem to be gaining popularity. One reason is that they involve engaging our students in the inquiry process. This gets students questioning and exploring the world around them. Most gifted children enjoy this method of lesson delivery. They have to solve problems and engage in more hands-on and meaningful scenarios compared to typical lesson delivery.

Science, Technology, Engineering, Arts, & Math-

This is just like STEM, but the arts are also integrated. Many students are interested, motivated by, or talented in the arts. STEAM takes all of the STEM learning and ensures the arts component is integrated into the learning choices and activities. Just Googling STEM or STEAM activities can lead to countless project ideas.

It is true that STEM and STEAM activities can require more materials and added costs for schools. Do not let this be a barrier. When parents and the community see the amazing projects and learning that can occur, many will want to help. Parent-teacher organizations are an excellent resource for schools. They can help reach out to other parents, the community, and businesses for donations and support. Holding career days, after-school activities, and events can allow the community to see what can be done and increase support. Start small, show what your students can do, and build from there.

Career & Technical Education-

Many do not consider CTE a program for our gifted population. They are wrong. These are not your old woodshop or basic trade school classes of previous generations. Depending on what is available in your area, students take courses in veterinary medicine, marketing, culinary arts, welding, or even aviation maintenance.

These programs provide hands-on, real-life courses for our students that they can find meaning in and, depending on the program, earn certifications and/or college credits. They are typically available at the high school level and can anchor a student's schedule to keep them motivated and engaged at the secondary level. Courses such as coding and computer programming have been shown to improve higher-level thinking, organization, and problem-solving skills.

If these programs are offered in your area, partnering with or creating them if you do not have them can be a great way to keep learning relevant for our high school-age students.

Are you implementing STEM/STEAM/CTE programs or services on your campus? How?

Brainstorm how you can start or increase these options for your students.

Life Skills

Children need life skills to become successful adults in the real world. Developing skills that help us improve interpersonal relationships, evaluate ourselves critically and realistically, and manage ourselves in various circumstances leads to progress and success. As obvious as some of these skills may be, they need to be taught to children in some manner. Here are five different skills that assist children in being happier and healthier. Many of these go hand in hand.

Decision Making

As individuals, we face decisions every day, sometimes every minute. Analyzing a situation using facts and considering one's values and belief system is essential for success and personal direction. Decision-making is complicated because it involves controlling feelings, actions, and behaviors before making a decision. This is no small feat! It can be difficult to do this, especially if external pressures are involved or personal goals are not fully developed.

Self-Awareness

Self-awareness is the ability to be aware of one's emotions, behavior, strengths, and challenges. With the many situations that we encounter every day, being "in touch with oneself" is not just a psychological cliché. Understanding how you respond to situations, people, and the level of your abilities is important. For example, if a student has test anxiety, and it makes them physically ill, then test-taking will always be a traumatic experience. However, if they understand that their reaction to tests has something to do with their fear of failure, they may be able to work through this challenge more easily. As a result, test-taking will become more bearable.

Problem Solving

All individuals need to be able to identify a problem and generate possible solutions, evaluating and selecting the best options. Problems come to us in many different forms. Students need to develop the skill set and confidence to tackle issues and choose what is right for them.

This is where critical thinking skills come into play. Critical thinking is gathering and evaluating information to make a thoughtful decision or arrive at a conclusion. This is often done by distinguishing relevance, the relationships between ideas, determining fact from opinion, and understanding the dichotomy between true or false statements. Imagine what would have happened if Troy had used some critical thinking with the Trojan horse!

We use divergent, convergent, and creative thinking skills to perform critical thinking. Divergent thinking involves a free form of thinking in which we brainstorm many possible answers or ideas for a particular issue. It does not always have a logical pattern and is based on what we know and do not know. If a family plans a vacation every year, involving family members in the planning by "brainstorming" different places to go not only emphasizes interpersonal skills but also lends to critical thinking.

Convergent thinking involves logically breaking down an issue into several components and arriving at a conclusion based on the best information available. This is also a part of critical thinking. For instance, if a classroom plans a party but realizes some students have food allergies, they may decide that a non-food-related party would be best.

Creative thinking involves creating something new with information at hand that fills in the gaps of the unknown. Creative thinking requires an ability to think out of the box and to see many different possibilities. If scientists had not done this with the Mars Rover, we would never have known the beauty of the red planet.

Critical thinking has several levels and is about innovation and making choices or developing ideas. Without it, we might stand perfectly still.

Empathy and sympathy are not always automatically acquired skills. Empathy is appreciating another person's feelings and perceptions and reacting accordingly. Sympathy is showing compassion or understanding for another person's situation. Many argue we cannot have one without the other. They appear to be imperative in our everyday lives, for if we lack one or the other, we will lack a moral compass or the ability to relate to other people. Our choices could become destructive for ourselves and others. Whether you agree or disagree that we need more or less empathy or sympathy, we do need our children and future generations to understand their fellow human beings.

Understanding that people have different views, values, talents, beliefs, and (*insert almost anything else here*) is not a bad thing. We should not be threatened by it. It is, indeed, a good thing. Seeing and understanding diverse thoughts and viewpoints increases our emotional intelligence and helps us function better in society. This is what we want in our children.

Interpersonal Skills

These skills are the ability to interact with others and value oneself. The ability to interact with social competence requires self-confidence, communication skills, active listening, and critical thinking. Socializing can be hard work! These skills are important in the school and workforce and the collaborations and interactions within these institutions. They are also important within the social circles we keep. One must know how to positively interact with others and overcome relationship difficulties. These skills help us determine the quality of individuals in our lives, and they lend to our self-worth and support systems. With children, it's important to teach them the qualities and characteristics of friendship. This should help them understand how to be a friend and determine if someone is truly a friend to them.

Our schools and parents need to keep life skills in mind as we teach and work with our students. These can be explicitly taught. They can also be incorporated into school activities and day-to-day talks between parents, teachers, and students.

Life Skills Incorporation Ideas

Look for ways to integrate life skills into your classroom!

1. Projects - Individual and group
   - Working together, meeting deadlines, what direction to take/focus on
2. History lessons and discussions
   - Decisions and consequences, successful people, discoveries
3. Science
   - Experiments, important scientists, discoveries
4. Analyzing character development
   - Novels, short stories, biographies, autobiographies
5. Math
   - How to use it in real life, use the concept to solve a problem in a group, how the given skill was developed

Twice-Exceptional Children - From Struggling to Thriving

Chapter 9

What are some ways you can encourage more life skills integration at your school?

What extracurricular activities does your school offer outside of the day to promote more hands-on learning?

How about activities that involve the community?

How can you help add more experiences for the students at your school?

Chapter 10
How Extra-Curricular Activities Can Help Us

All over and as much as can be provided.

Extracurricular activities can provide transitional recreation services that help build independence in classroom settings, including those that support leisure and social skills. Benefits may be gained from after-school programs, summer camps, community programs, etc. It is helpful for twice-exceptional students to find success in multiple areas. Activities outside of the classroom are vital for real-world learning and build self-confidence as well as socialization skills.

Some extracurricular programs may address a student's academic, communication, vocational, or social goals and can be included in an educational plan.

Art and Music

Art and music can provide therapeutic outlets for communicating thoughts and feelings. Creativity can be expressed in many different forms by all types of students. Allowing a student to demonstrate knowledge of a subject creatively empowers them and will enable educators to understand what the person truly knows.

Music has been known to increase executive functioning by providing training through rhythm and performance. Through regular practice of an instrument or voice, a healthy routine may be established. Many 2e students can express themselves creatively through different forms of music.

Performing Arts

Acting and drama have many academic, social, and collaborative benefits for 2e students. Critical analysis of a production and script can provide a deeper understanding of the author's characters, message, and purpose. Multiple script readings can help build fluency, accuracy, vocabulary development, and intonation. Acting can provide an opportunity for students to express themselves artistically and can help build confidence and tenacity. Collaborating with other children through teamwork in the performing arts often helps improve communication and interpersonal relationships.

Improvisation is also an excellent activity for students if the teacher is sensitive to shy participants. Actual improv is a collaborative effort where all participants can have fun and appreciate each other's creativity.

Sports/Athletics

Engagement in sports can lead to a better self-image and an improved understanding of collaboration and teamwork. Sports can assist students in learning new skills, including visual-spatial and even mathematical, while they enjoy the benefits of exercise and relaxation. Participating in sports can aid in social-emotional development as well. Competitive sports can foster a growth mindset by allowing students to learn through mistakes. Team sports are also valuable in adding teamwork skills and relationship building.

Implementing the arts into your lessons can shake things up, bring other skills and modalities into play, and allow all students to show their learning in different ways. The arts are also a great way to teach resiliency, self-reliance, relaxation, and mindfulness. Please see our resources section for information on the book <u>Teacher's Guide to Resiliency Through The Arts</u>. This is an excellent resource for any teacher wanting to bring creative skills and the arts into their classroom.

Chapter 10

What opportunities do students have at your school to participate in the arts and sports daily or at least regularly?

What activities are available outside of the school day? Is there a wide range of options and availability to all students?

Are the activities at your school focused on the students' wants and needs? Are they inclusive?

What can you do as a classroom teacher or school leader to increase the integration of arts and activities in your classroom(s)?

Chapter 11
The Importance of Mindfulness and Social & Emotional Supports

Twice-exceptional children can have social and emotional issues that interfere with their ability to make friends and sustain social relationships. These issues can prevent them from providing themselves with self-care and to manage themselves successfully in stressful situations.

In addition to this, 2e students may have emotional issues tied to their academic and social challenges, such as feelings of failure, depression, anger, isolation, self-harm, and, in extreme cases, suicide. Students need tools to overcome these issues. Opportunities to develop a healthy self-awareness, identify their vulnerabilities, and interact with other students who share their struggles are often helpful.

This can be done through:

1. Journaling and Creating Positive Rituals

Start a morning or evening routine by participating in relaxation exercises, goal setting, or inspirational activities, along with identifying one's current state of mind and needs. This could be done by writing questions or affirmations about oneself in a journal. Looking back on some of the entries and celebrating current accomplishments from past ideas can increase positivity.

2. Maintain Emotional Well-Being

Provide oneself with opportunities for meditation, or mind-clearing, as this can be an emotionally cleansing experience. Watching the sunset, participating in breathing exercises, sitting outside, coloring, or listening to the wind are all great activities for this. Surrounding oneself with supportive, positive people is also vital to maintaining mental stability, as is minimizing interactions with critical or negative peers.

3. Self-Check-In

During the day, provide oneself with a check-in and assess current feelings.

Ask these questions:

· What are you thinking?

· Are you having physical reactions to stress or thoughts?

· What could you do to minimize any negative feelings or thoughts?

All of these can be done at home or in the classroom. Just taking a "Mindful Moment" when students come in from lunch or PE can profoundly change the energy in the classroom. Students do not have to meditate; simply taking one or two full minutes to close their eyes and clear their minds is a great mental break. You can even use a chime, a singing bowl, or a peaceful melody to start the moment.

Another tool is to use seating and tactile objects to support fidgeting and help with focus. These can be stress balls, glitter sticks, or other tactile sensory toys (easily found online) to help with fidgeting. Purchasing or making wiggle seats, allowing students to sit on yoga balls, and using standing desks (or something as simple as two cut tennis balls to place on chair feet, allowing a quiet way to wiggle) can help students focus. Large rubber bands can even be placed on chair legs to allow feet and legs to bounce quietly. Using accommodations shows you are open to ensuring they are comfortable and ready to learn.

Many of these tools will help children focus. If you are worried about them becoming toys, you can have that conversation and say they will lose the privilege of using them for a while if they become a distraction. Once the novelty wears off, the initial issues will fade.

Please Don't Forget That…
You are important too!

Being an educator is challenging and stressful. In recent years, research has begun to show the effects of Secondary Impact Trauma. This occurs when people interact with others who have been through trauma, and the act of caring and supporting those who have been traumatized begins to affect the caretakers.

Nurses and law enforcement agents suffer from Secondary Impact Trauma at high rates, but teachers are impacted the most. Even before the pandemic, millions of children came to school having been impacted by poverty or abuse, among other injustices. These things can unknowingly impact the mental health of teachers as well.

Your mental state and stability are just as important as your students' well-being. Stress and fatigue significantly impact your emotional and physical health, and you must treat yourself with kindness and self-respect. Here are a few ideas to achieve your inner peace and balance:

1. Practice deep breathing and meditation
2. Take a warm shower or use a warm compress on the forehead
3. Listen to music or walk in nature
4. Read a book or watch a movie
5. Get a massage
6. Spend time with people you love
7. Take a break from news and technology
8. Learn to leave work at work.

Chapter 11

Book Study & Reflection Questions

How will you empower your students to have more say in how they learn and their learning environment?

What "tools" can you provide your students to help them focus?

What are some ways you can support your own mental health?

Chapter 12
Above All Else: Don't Forget That I Am Gifted First!

As previously noted, if a 2e child is identified for support, it is most likely for help in their area(s) of challenge. Most school systems focus resources on identifying and supporting struggling students. A 2e student's high abilities can be overlooked with this deficit-based focus.

In many schools, support for an area of challenge is the only specific support students are provided. How will children excel if their area of strength is not nurtured?

A note from Adam – My first year of teaching was as a reading intervention teacher. Since I was new, I did what I was told and ran the program as it had always been done. The program was to support middle school students who were reading below grade level.

I had, and continue to have, concerns over how these programs are structured. The problem is that my intervention was during the student's elective class period. This meant that, instead of attending an elective of their choice, students would come to my classroom for extra reading support.

Just imagine if you were a child in this position. You are struggling in a particular area, and to "help you," we take you out of the class you enjoy. During this time, you do more work in the subject where you struggle the most. This seems like more of a punishment than a benefit to the child. What does this do to a child's motivation in school, especially for a child with a significant learning disability, as a 2e student might have?

Twice-exceptional children are gifted too. They have at least one area or talent in which they excel and one or more areas of disability. Both areas must be addressed to help these children succeed. Remember, 2e children are green, a distinct combination of yellow (strengths) and blue (disabilities).

In an ideal school district, the gifted and special education leaders work closely to support these students. In fact, in some districts, a child's giftedness comes first. What does this mean? It means a student is placed into gifted services and programming according to their needs. Special education then provides support within the gifted program structure. What does this look like?

There are many examples, and every school is different. One example may be quantitatively gifted children who excel in math but struggle with reading. These students can "walk up" to the next grade level for math for part of the school day, but the special education teacher can support their English Language Arts period in the classroom for reading. These children can excel in math, the area of strength, and get the reading support they need. Students can feel fulfilled and successful in their domains of strength.

Where to Start?

- If this is not happening at your school, either as a parent or educator, you should ask questions.

- Next, start talking with your colleagues and see who notices the same needs you do. Together, you can start planning change.

- Make sure to do some research. Use facts to show the needs of this population.

- Also, don't forget to give examples of former students you know who were 2e or may have been, and talk about what they experienced. We all want to help our students; the debate might be about how.

Chapter 12

Book Study & Reflection Questions

Are some students receiving special education services also receiving gifted services at your school? Reflect.

Can you think of any students who probably should be receiving these students?

If you are not seeing some students in both special education programs and gifted services at your school, you might need to start asking some questions. Who can you ask to see if some 2e students are being missed?

What can you do for these specific students if they are in your classroom?

References, Articles, & Resources

Books –

Gifted Children & How Trauma Impacts Them: 20 Things Gifted Children Wish Their Teachers and Parents Understood
Adam C. Laningham, Dr. Melissa Sadin, & Nathan Levy, 2019

C for Curiosity
Lin Lim, Ph.D., 2022

Teachers' Guide to Trauma: 20 Things Kids with Trauma Wish Their Teachers Knew
Dr. Melissa Sadin & Nathan Levy, 2019

A Parent's Guide to Gifted Children
James T. Webb, Janet L. Gore, Edward R. Amend, & Arlene R. DeVries, 2007

Teacher's Guide to Resiliency Through The Arts
Cally Flox, Melisa Sadin, & Nathan Levy, 2019

Differentiation for Gifted Learners: Going Beyond the Basics,
Diane Heacox & Richard M. Cash, 2020

The Power of Self-Advocacy for Gifted Learners: Teaching the Four Essential Steps to Success
Deb Douglas, 2017

What to do When Your Kid is Smarter Than You
Linda Levitt, 2007

Multiple Intelligences in the Elementary Classroom: A Teachers Toolkit
Susan Baum, Julie Viens, & Barbara Slatin, 2005

Understanding Twice-exceptional Learners: Connecting Research to Practice
Matthew Fugate, Wendy Behrens, & Cecelia Boswell, 2020

Twice Exceptional: Supporting and Educating Bright and Creative Students with Learning Difficulties
Scott Barry Kaufman (Ed.), 2018

Ungifted: Intelligence Redefined
Scott Barry Kaufman, 2015

The Explosive Child
Dr. Ross Greene, 2014

**To Be Gifted and Learning Disabled:
Strength-Based Strategies for Helping Twice-
Exceptional Students With LD, ADHD, ASD,
and More**

Susan M. Baum, Robin Schader, & Steven
Owen, 2017

Web Resources & Articles –

The
official website for this book and our series. We will be continually adding updated information, resources, and presentations.
**https://brightchildbooks.com/collections/gifte
d-struggling_twice-exceptional**

www.zenliving.com

SENG - Supporting Emotional
Needs of the Gifted
www.sengifted.org

Bridges Graduate School of Cognitive Diversity in Education - Certificate, Master's and Doctoral Program

https://graduateschool.bridges.edu/

www.2enews.com and Variations 2e magazine are focused on providing the latest news, research, and perspectives on how best to support the needs of this population of learners.

Bridges 2e Center: Strength-based assessment to supplement IEP or 504 plan. Free resources, including monthly crucial conversations around 2e topics.
https://2ecenter.org/

Ten tips for Teaching Twice-Exceptional Students ASCD
http://www.ascd.org/publications/newsletters/education_update/nov13/vol55/num11/Ten_Tips_for_Teaching_the_Twice-Exceptional_Student.aspx

Strategies for Supporting Students who are Twice-Exceptional. *The Journal of Special Education.*

https://files.eric.ed.gov/fulltext/EJ1185416.pdf

2eminds. Quick and Easy Mindfulness Practices **https://www.2eminds.com/mindfulness-parenting-twice-exceptional-2e-children/**

www.gifteddevelopment.org

The Columbus Organization
www.columbusorg.com

National Association for Gifted Children-
www.nagc.org

Your state Gifted Association

We also want to thank Jamie Dana again for her insight and contribution to Chapter 11 of our What Parents Need to Know book.

Elevate Counseling
admin@elevatecounselingaz.com
https://elevatecounselingaz.com

About the Authors

Adam Chase Laningham, M.Ed
Author, Consultant, and
Founder of Bright Child AZ &
The Gifted Collective

Adam Laningham, author of Gifted Children & How Trauma Impacts Them, and Thinkology 2.0, has over 20 years of experience in the field of education. Adam was recognized as the Arizona Gifted Teacher of the Year. He has taught at several schools in multiple grade levels, created and facilitated numerous gifted programs, and also served as a district gifted services manager coordinating programs for over 6000 gifted students.

Adam has served on the Board of Directors for the Arizona Association for Gifted & Talented for many years and is currently the President of SENG (Supporting Emotional Needs of the Gifted). As founder and owner of Bright Child AZ, Adam is an international speaker, consultant, and gifted advocate.

brightchildbooks.com

adam@brightchildbooks.com

BRIGHT CHILD BOOKS, LLC
BrightChildAZ.com
BOOKS, PUBLISHING, & MORE

GIFTED CHILDREN
& HOW TRAUMA IMPACTS THEM

THINKology 2.0

About the Authors

Val Wilson, M.Ed
Author, Consultant, School
Gifted Specialist & Adventurer

Val holds a Masters in Curriculum and Instruction, along with several certifications and endorsements in gifted learners, elementary education, adult education, reading, ELA, ESL, and math. Val has been teaching for over three decades and currently works as a gifted specialist and coach for a Title I School. She is also a Multi-Tiered System of Support Coordinator and a Professional Learning Community Facilitator for Science and Social Studies at her school. Val has taught instructional techniques for various learners at the college and professional development level over the past seven years, both online and in person.

In her spare time, Val serves as the appointed Public Art Commissioner of the City of Youngtown, AZ, who recruits and supports local gifted artists. She is also CEO of Veldazio Rudolpho, her artwork design label and company.

"The energy of the mind is the essence of life."
– Aristotle

About the Authors

Lin Lim, Ph.D.
Author, Dean of Graduate Students, Translational Human Development Scientist

Lin Lim is the Dean of Students and Communications at Bridges Graduate School of Cognitive Diversity in Education (BGS). She holds a doctorate in psychology from Boston University, an Academic Graduate Certificate in Mind, Brain, and Education (Johns Hopkins University), and an Academic Graduate Certificate in 2e Education (BGS). Her current interests include interdisciplinary embodied complex dynamic systems thinking and practical applications around positive parenting, education, school-workplace transitions, and human development. She founded **Quark Collaboration Institute**, a non-profit focusing on human dignity and well-being across the lifespan. She serves on the boards of several gifted-related non-profits - Supporting the Emotional Needs of the Gifted (**SENG**), National Association for Gifted Children Parent Editorial Content and Advisory Board, Gifted Homeschoolers Forum (**GHF**), **Gifted Education Family Network**, and **PGRetreat.org**.

Zenliving.com

"I suppose the one quality in an astronaut more powerful than any other is curiosity. They have to get some place nobody's ever been." Astronaut John Glenn

The Books in our Series

Twice-Exceptional Children - From Struggling to Thriving

What Parents Need To Know 2023/24	*What Educators Need To Know* 2023/24
Essential 2e Teaching Strategies That Are Also Good For All Learners 2024	*What School Administrators Need to Know* 2025
What School Mental Health Professionals Need To Know 2025	

Our book series allows for positive collaborations between all stakeholders through a consistent use of conceptual definitions, philosophy, pedagogy, and applications. This allows for a common starting point to understand, communicate, and serve students' needs holistically through robust discussions between stakeholders. What happens at home impacts the school, and the reverse is also true.

Main points of the series

1. Lead with gifts - your child is gifted first!

2. A twice-exceptional learner always shows an interaction between high abilities (yellow) and complex challenges (blue). Using Susan Baum and colleagues' color metaphor, a 2e child is always green (yellow interacting with blue).

3. The NEST! Perspective is a human development guiding framework to nurture sustainable growth and well-being across our developmental lifespan.

Ask us about our workshops, consulting, professional development, & events!

We love working with groups and ensure every workshop and event is tailored to the group's needs. Please let us know how we can support you!

You can contact us at:
adam@brightchildbooks.com

Books in our Trauma Support Series

BRIGHT CHILD BOOKS, LLC
BrightChildAZ.com
BOOKS, PUBLISHING, & MORE

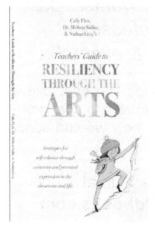

Made in the USA
Las Vegas, NV
15 August 2024